The Jesus Bible

STUDY SERIES

REVOLT

THE STORY OF GOD'S PURSUIT OF IMPERFECT PEOPLE

Aaron Coe, Ph.D.
Series Writer & General Editor of *The Jesus Bible*

Matt Rogers, Ph.D.
Series Writer & Lead Writer of *The Jesus Bible*

Harper*Christian* Resources

passionpublishing

The Jesus Bible Study Series: Revolt
© 2023 by Passion Publishing

Requests for information should be addressed to:
HarperChristian Resources, 3900 Sparks Dr. SE, Grand Rapids, Michigan 49546

ISBN 978-0-310-15500-3 (softcover)
ISBN 978-0-310-15501-0 (ebook)

All Scripture quotations are from The Holy Bible, New International Version®, NIV®. Copyright © 1973, 1978, 1984, 2011 by Biblica, Inc.® Used by permission of Zondervan. All rights reserved worldwide. www.zondervan.com. The "NIV" and "New International Version" are trademarks registered in the United States Patent and Trademark Office by Biblica, Inc.™

Any internet addresses (websites, blogs, etc.) and telephone numbers in this book are offered as a resource. They are not intended in any way to be or imply an endorsement by HarperChristian Resources, nor does HarperChristian Resources vouch for the content of these sites and numbers for the life of this book.

HarperChristian Resources titles may be purchased in bulk for church, business, fundraising, or ministry use. For information, please e-mail ResourceSpecialist@ChurchSource.com.

First printing February 2023 / Printed in the United States of America

CONTENTS

Introduction v

Lesson 1: **The Fall** 1

Lesson 2: **The Curse** 17

Lesson 3: **Sin Nature** 31

Lesson 4: **Completely Broken** 43

Lesson 5: **Systems of Evil** 59

Lesson 6: **Glimmers of Hope** 73

Leader's Guide 89

About the Authors 93

INTRODUCTION

Have you ever noticed that most movies follow the same basic story?

After meeting the main characters, we are introduced to the tension that the plot of the movie is going to work toward resolving. Something goes wrong—the model marriage starts to unravel; the dream vacation hits a snag; the diamond stash is raided by an unknown group of assassins. Whatever the tension, it drives the story. Everything that follows seeks to fix the problem and put things back together in a way that is beautiful, whole, and right.

The story of the Bible is much the same, except this narrative chronicles God's true story. The first two chapters of the book of Genesis introduce us to the key details of the Bible's grand story. We meet God—revealed in three persons: Father, Son, and Holy Spirit—who designs and crafts all things so his creation can display how great he is. We also meet men and women who are created in God's image to reflect him throughout the earth. The purpose of creation is that God's fame, his praise, will fill the entire earth.

But from this pristine beginning tragedy is birthed. God's people rebel against him, reject his authority, and usher sin into the world. The tension of that revolt is the theme of this study. In the pages that follow, we are going to consider the tragedy of sin, starting with humanity's disobedience in the Garden, the curse that God gives as a result, and the way that sin shapes the world in which we live. Throughout the entire journey, you'll see consistent hints of the work of Jesus Christ and God's miraculous plan to save sinners and fix the world.

As a reminder, this is the second "act" in God's beautiful overarching story told throughout the Bible: (1) *Beginnings*, (2) *Revolt*, (3) *People*, (4) *Savior*, (5) *Church*, (6) *Forever.* Every detail in each story found within the pages of the Bible could be placed within one of these six acts, which tell God's story from Genesis to Revelation. This act, *Revolt,* is vital for our understanding of God's mission because it answers two vital questions. First, "What went wrong?" And second, "Why did it go wrong?" It also sets the stage for the coming acts that will help us see how we try to fix the situation, as well as what God is going to do to right these wrongs through Jesus Christ.

Revolt will push you to dig deeper into Scripture and discover God's truth for yourself. At times, you will be asked to apply some aspect of God's story to your own story through reflection questions. Read *Revolt* ready to engage your mind and your heart. Our prayer is that as you do, the study will prove to be far more than just another weekly task to add to your calendar. Although the topic is tragic, it will help you understand the depth of human sin so you can make sense of the complexity of your struggles and the fallen world in which we live.

Most importantly, a consideration of the *Revolt* of God's people in the Bible will reveal the magnificent scope of the Lord's love, shown through the person and work of Jesus Christ.

Lesson 1

THE FALL

Now the serpent was more crafty than any of the wild animals the Lᴏʀᴅ God had made. He said to the woman, "Did God really say, 'You must not eat from any tree in the garden'?"

GENESIS 3:1

You who boast in the law, do you dishonor God by breaking the law?

ROMANS 2:23

[God] leads out the
prisoners with singing;
but the rebellious live in
a sun-scorched land.

— PSALM 68:6

WELCOME

Our family recently experienced a major heartbreak. My wife and I have four children, two biologically born and two through adoption. We also had a fifth child that we "adopted," though not legally speaking. Tanya was nineteen when she entered our family. For eight years she was almost always with us. She went with us on family vacations, attended church with us, and joined us for family meals. She even lived in our basement for a time.

One night, while recovering from a medical procedure, Tanya unexpectedly passed away at twenty-seven years old. To this day, there are no clear answers for how she died. The best guess is a blood clot. Needless to say, we were (and still are) in shock. We are grieving. We are sad and are reminded that this world is broken. This world is not how it should be.

A simple look around today's world quickly reveals that something is very wrong. A global pandemic. Famine in third-world countries. War raging across the globe. A tragic car crash that kills young people going to college. Cancer for a mom of four children. Poverty. Racism. On and on the list could go. All of us could make a list of injustices that are evident in our lives.

Regardless of what you believe is the source of life's problems—whether it be political, financial, or sociological—one thing is certain: *something is badly broken*. Although our social media feeds are filled with incessant chatter about solutions to society's problems, the world around us doesn't seem to be getting any better. In fact, most days, it feels like things are actually getting worse.

The Bible doesn't hide the fact that life is full of pain and suffering. God didn't give us simplistic answers to the complexity of our reality. In fact, the Bible is brutally honest about the depth of the brokenness in our world and provides an answer as to why society became such a mess in the first place. These answers all point forward to the great hope found in Jesus Christ.

1. What would you say is your biggest frustration about our world today?

2. Do you have a hard time reconciling the brokenness of the world? Why or why not?

READ

The tragic story begins in the third chapter of Genesis. Right on the heels of the stunning description of God's creation—which crescendos with the design of men and women who are tasked with cultivating God's world and filling the earth with His image-bearing worshipers—comes the tale of creation and humanity's unraveling due to Adam and Eve's sin and disobedience. Pick any book in the Bible and you are sure to see story after story that testify to the effects of this fall and the universal problem among humans that it brought.

In many ways, this just seems to be how life goes. A good day filled with happiness can end with a phone call announcing a tragedy. Hours of confident preparation for a test sometimes result in a lower grade than anticipated. A new relationship that brought such hope for lasting joy ends in a broken engagement. Pain often seems to follow joy.

But it didn't have to be this way! Men and women were designed to celebrate God's goodness in the perfect world that He created. But in one fatal act, Adam and Eve plunged the world into the depth of chaos. Here is how the story reads in Genesis:

> ¹ *Now the serpent was more crafty than any of the wild animals the* Lord *God had made. He said to the woman, "Did God really say, 'You must not eat from any tree in the garden'?"*
>
> ² *The woman said to the serpent, "We may eat fruit from the trees in the garden,* ³ *but God did say, 'You must not eat fruit from the tree that is in the middle of the garden, and you must not touch it, or you will die.'"*
>
> ⁴ *"You will not certainly die," the serpent said to the woman.* ⁵ *"For God knows that when you eat from it your eyes will be opened, and you will be like God, knowing good and evil."*
>
> ⁶ *When the woman saw that the fruit of the tree was good for food and pleasing to the eye, and also desirable for gaining wisdom, she took some and ate it. She*

also gave some to her husband, who was with her, and he ate it. [7] Then the eyes of both of them were opened, and they realized they were naked; so they sewed fig leaves together and made coverings for themselves.

Genesis 3:1–7

The story of the fall is fairly straightforward. Satan, in the form of a serpent, tempts Adam and Eve to disobey God. They give in to his deception and eat fruit from the tree of good and evil that God had told them to avoid. This act seems fairly minor in the big scheme of things. After all, it was just a little piece of fruit, right? Who really cares?

God! In his grand story, this seemingly minor act is nothing short of an outright revolt against His plan, design, and goodness. Of course, the fact this happened was no surprise to God. In his eternal knowledge, he knew that humankind would sin. He already had a plan in place to save them and fix the problems they had brought into his perfect world through Jesus Christ. This is why Jesus is the focus of the entire Bible.

3.   Why do you think Adam and Eve chose to listen to the enemy's lies?

4. How does the enemy whisper in your ear to get you to doubt God's goodness?

REFLECT

The Nature of the Revolt: Denying God's Plan

For our purposes, it's vital to understand the nature of this revolt so we can better grasp the extent of God's love through Jesus.

First, we see that Satan questioned God's wisdom and asked Adam and Eve to deny God's plan using the subtle question, "Did God really say?" (Genesis 3:1). God's command certainly may have seemed arbitrary to the first couple. Why was this one tree off limits? Why would they die if they ate of its fruit? God didn't attempt to answer these questions in the first two chapters of Genesis. He simply gave his word to his people and expected them to obey—and they didn't. They disobeyed God, which is, at the core, the most basic definition of sin. *Sin is disobedience to God and his word.* Read what Paul writes:

> [17] *Now you, if you call yourself a Jew; if you rely on the law and boast in God;* [18] *if you know his will and approve of what is superior because you are instructed by the law;* [19] *if you are convinced that you are a guide for the blind, a light for those who are in the dark,* [20] *an instructor of the foolish, a teacher of little children, because you have in the law the embodiment of knowledge and truth—*

21 you, then, who teach others, do you not teach yourself? You who preach against stealing, do you steal? 22 You who say that people should not commit adultery, do you commit adultery? You who abhor idols, do you rob temples? 23 You who boast in the law, do you dishonor God by breaking the law? 24 As it is written: "God's name is blasphemed among the Gentiles because of you."

Romans 2:17–24

5. Which of God's commands in your life seems most arbitrary to you? Why?

6. When and how are you most tempted to question God's plan?

The Nature of the Revolt: Undermining God's Choice

Adam and Eve undermined God's design with their choice to disobey. As Creator, God knows how we are intended to function. He knows what is good and best for us and what we should avoid. He knows what is going to bring us harm and what will cause us to flourish. We are created to humbly submit to his design, not to come out from under his rule and make decisions that we feel are best. This is exactly what Adam and Eve did. They saw the fruit was "good for food and pleasing to the eye, and also desirable for gaining wisdom" (Genesis 3:6). In Eve's mind, it made sense to eat the fruit, regardless of what God had clearly said.

Sin is always like that. We commit sins because the actions are appealing—they seem wise in the moment, they make us feel good, and they are attractive to our eyes and hearts. If sins were clearly nauseating, it's unlikely that most of us would pursue them. But, apart from the grace of God and the mind of Christ, we often don't see sin as evil. We sin because we want sin more than we want God, which is exactly the choice Adam and Eve made so long ago in the Garden. Here is another way to think about sin: *Sin is loving something more than God.*

The apostle Paul described sin as exchanging "the truth about God for a lie" and worshiping and serving "created things rather than the Creator" (Romans 1:25). Paul says the heart of all human sin is an *exchange*. We all were created to love God and worship him, but we give up that worship in order to love something else—like a relationship, money, power, sports, fame . . . the list goes on. Anything can take God's place in our hearts and minds and cause us to abandon his worshipful design for our lives.

7. Where are you most tempted to worship something other than God as God? Why?

8. What are some of the triggers that cause you to distrust God's way?

The Nature of the Revolt: Rebelling Against God's Goodness

Perhaps the worst part of Adam and Eve's story is the fact that they rebelled against God's goodness, kindness, and love. Think about this. They had been intricately fashioned by God, placed in a perfect world, and given everything they needed to survive and thrive. God also saw that it was not good for either Adam or Eve to be alone, so he gave them the gift of relationships (see Genesis 2:18). Most importantly, they knew and were known fully by God!

The Creator of the universe walked with them in the cool of the Garden and met their every need (see 3:8). There was only one thing off limits. One tree and its fruit. They were given access to everything else! They had all the other trees, not to mention the amazing beauty they could enjoy simply by being in God's presence and feasting on the bountiful delights that he provided. By choosing to embrace what God told them to shun—namely, the fruit of that one tree—they revealed their doubt in God's goodness and his care for their needs. It seemed that God was holding out on them or keeping them from something really good.

We often entertain those same questions when we sin. We may not say them out loud, but our actions reveal that we believe lies about God and question his goodness in our lives. Telling even "little white lies" to get ahead at work or school reveals that we doubt if God can truly meet our needs. Unwise relationships demonstrate that we question if God is wise and capable leading us to a loving relationship in his time and his way.

This idea reveals our third and final way of thinking about sin: *sin is believing lies about God.* Adam and Eve's sinful choice served as the prototype for all subsequent human sin. The reality is that we are not all that creative with our sins. Not much has changed in the thousands of years that have gone by since this tragic scene in the Garden of Eden. We still sin by disobeying God and His word, by loving something more than God, and by believing lies about God. All of our foolish choices come from those same sources, as the following passages relate:

All of us have become like one who is unclean, and all our righteous acts are like filthy rags; we all shrivel up like a leaf, and like the wind our sins sweep us away.

Isaiah 64:6

For the wages of sin is death, but the gift of God is eternal life in Christ Jesus our Lord.

Romans 6:23

As for you, you were dead in your transgressions and sins, in which you used to live when you followed the ways of this world and of the ruler of the kingdom of the air, the spirit who is now at work in those who are disobedient. All of us also lived among them at one time, gratifying the cravings of our flesh and following its desires and thoughts. Like the rest, we were by nature deserving of wrath.

Ephesians 2:1–3

Everyone who sins breaks the law; in fact, sin is lawlessness.

1 John 3:4

Sin is not a little thing. With every sinful action we take and choice we make, we revolt against our Creator and his mission in our world. Rather than submitting to God's loving care, we decide to live for ourselves and become masters of our own lives. But the reality is that we are horrible at living lives under our own domain. We run headlong after our own passions and priorities, only to find that we're not actually all that great at being in charge of our own lives—a lesson that Adam and Eve also had to learn the hard way.

Those who know and love Jesus understand this reality. We all make bad gods of our own lives. He is far better at leading our lives than we are at creating our own reality.

9. Reread Genesis 3:7–13. What are the ways the first couple responded to sin?

10. How can you relate to Adam and Eve's experience when it comes to your sin?

CLOSE

So, what do we do with our sin? This was the challenge that Adam and Eve faced. The Bible is clear that the moment they sinned, "the eyes of both of them were opened" (Genesis 3:7). Adam and Eve saw their heinous sin for what it was and knew that they had blown it.

Have you ever been there? Of course! We all have. In the moment, a sinful choice seems to make so much sense. It's almost like we can't help but go down a path we know we should not walk. Then, when we step across the line, the sin lets us down. This is what sin does: it overpromises and underdelivers. It says it will provide us will happiness, fulfillment, and hope—but it takes far more than it gives. We end up with shame, guilt, condemnation, and despair.

Adam and Eve's first response when they realized they had sinned was to try to cover themselves because of the shame they felt. Before they sinned, they were naked and unashamed. But now, because of their sin, they felt exposed. So they sewed fig leaves together and made "coverings for themselves" to try to hide their shame (verse 7).

Today, our "fig leaves" look much different than those worn by Adam and Eve, but we are all still guilty of trying to hide our shame. Some of us believe that hard work will somehow mask the sins lurking in our hearts. Others among us run to religion, steeped in rules of how to be "right," in an attempt to cover our sin by being good—often in a hypocritical way that makes us outwardly look righteous while inside we are hiding a perverted heart. Whatever our "leaves" of choice are, the reality is that we all try to hide our shame.

Adam and Eve's next response when they realized they had sinned was to try to hide from God (see verse 8). The story in Genesis portrays a comical scene. Can you imagine the two ducking behind a bush in a remote corner of the Garden, hoping the Creator of the universe would not be able to find them? It's the worst game of hide-and-seek ever. God was going to find them. But we are no different. We still love to try to hide from God! We hope that if we just lay low, God will ignore us and overlook our rebellion against him. Maybe he will forget—or maybe if enough time passes, he won't think our sin is such a big deal anymore.

God's story contains one more response to sin. After Adam lost the hide-and-seek game, God called him out and held him accountable for eating the fruit. How did Adam respond? He did what almost every person does when he or she gets busted. He blamed someone else. First, he blamed Eve—or, more specifically, blamed God for giving him Eve (see verse 12). Then Eve blamed her failure on the serpent. Rather than owning their sin, Adam and Eve both blamed someone or something else, hoping their finger-pointing would free them from punishment.

Sin is the reason for all of life's suffering. The world is broken because of sin. Try as we might, we cannot escape sin's death grip on our lives or in our world. Shame, hiding, and blame only heighten the problem. One thing is certain: the answer to humanity's predicament would not come from sinful people. The only way to escape sin's power would be through God's power and through his plan. The rest of the Bible will describe that plan, clearly showing us God's design to save sinners and fix the world through the person and work of Jesus Christ.

11. Name a few times in your life when you have tried to hide something from someone else or shift the blame. How did that work out?

12. Why is Jesus, and not a human agent, the only answer to humanity's sin problem?

Lesson 2

THE CURSE

"Because you have done this, 'Cursed are you above all livestock and all wild animals! You will crawl on your belly and you will eat dust all the days of your life.'"

GENESIS 3:14

God gave them over to a depraved mind, so that they do what ought not to be done.

ROMANS 1:28

They will have to give
account to him who is
ready to judge the
living and the dead.

— 1 PETER 4:5

WELCOME

All in all, I was a pretty good kid growing up, but there were a few moments that gave my parents some gray hairs. Like the time my friend and I decided we needed to put an active fireplace in our treehouse. Or the time I fell through the ice on a frozen pond after repeatedly being told not to walk on it. You probably remember a time as a child when you disobeyed your parents or a teacher and got caught. Maybe you broke a rule you didn't like or touched something off limits that you found too compelling to resist. But then you got caught.

Even now, you might be replaying that episode in your mind and shuddering at what happened next. That feeling of terror as your eyes met those of your parents' and you waited for their response. The shrill yell of the teacher as she commanded you to go to the principal's office. There is nothing worse than knowing that judgment is coming . . . and that you deserve whatever is going to happen next.

Imagine how Adam and Eve must have felt. They had disobeyed God in spite of his great love for them. Not only had they broken God's law, but they were also now awaiting the consequences from the One who had just recently spoken all things—including them—into existence. Certainly, someone with the power to make the world had the power to judge severely. They cowered in fear at the voice of the God they had once worshiped with joy.

1. What do you think Adam and Eve were thinking and feeling before God responded to their sin?

2. What was likely going through their minds as they hid from God?

READ

The Nature of God's Justice

Before we consider the judgment that God eventually gives to Adam and Eve, we might wonder why he even needs to judge at all. He is God, after all. Couldn't he simply pretend that Adam and Eve hadn't done anything wrong? Couldn't he just act like a kind grandfather trying to discipline his cute two-year-old granddaughter—and fail at doing so? Couldn't he just overlook Adam and Eve's misbehavior and go on as if nothing had happened?

Such an idea undermines a key aspect of God's character. He is a just God, which means he always does what is right. A grandfather might be doing what he thinks is loving when he excuses his granddaughter's clear rebellion, but he is not doing what is just. His granddaughter's actions were not just, even if he chooses to overlook them. If he goes on to give her a milkshake instead of discipline, he is living up to the stereotype of a gracious grandparent—loving at the expense of doing what is just, which isn't really love.

God is not like our fictitious grandparent. He is always loving and always just. He can't turn off a key aspect of His character—a part of what makes him God—to overlook the consequences of sin. He had already told Adam and Eve what would happen if they ate the forbidden fruit: "When you eat from it you will certainly die" (Genesis 2:17). God had said they would die, and since he is a just God—a God who always keeps his word—he had to do exactly what he said he would do. Adam and Eve had to die. This is the verdict that God rendered:

¹⁴ So the L ORD God said to the serpent, "Because you have done this,

> "Cursed are you above all livestock
>   and all wild animals!
> You will crawl on your belly
>   and you will eat dust
>   all the days of your life.
> ¹⁵ And I will put enmity
>   between you and the woman,
>   and between your offspring and hers;
> he will crush your head,
>   and you will strike his heel."

¹⁶ To the woman he said,

> "I will make your pains in childbearing very severe;
>   with painful labor you will give birth to children.
> Your desire will be for your husband,
>   and he will rule over you."

¹⁷ To Adam he said, "Because you listened to your wife and ate fruit from the tree about which I commanded you, 'You must not eat from it,'

> "Cursed is the ground because of you;
>   through painful toil you will eat food from it
>   all the days of your life.
> ¹⁸ It will produce thorns and thistles for you,
>   and you will eat the plants of the field.

[19] By the sweat of your brow
    you will eat your food
until you return to the ground,
    since from it you were taken;
for dust you are
    and to dust you will return."

Genesis 3:14–19

3. Does it frustrate or encourage you that God is always just? Explain your response.

4. What stands out to you in the curse given to Satan (the serpent), Eve, and Adam? Does this list of punishments seem unreasonable or unfair to you? Explain your response.

The Nature of Our Rebellion

If we're not careful, we can trick ourselves into thinking the world is primarily good with a few bad actors sprinkled in. However, it is much worse. Because of the first couple's sin, the whole world order was flipped. We are all living in the effects of their rebellion. Everything on earth, since the Fall, has been tainted. As a result, nothing remains as it was once intended.

The verses you just read are commonly known as the "curse" because they portray the depth of God's anger toward the revolt. God first cursed Satan for his deception and said he would crawl on his belly the rest of his days. God then issued a curse against the woman, saying she would experience pain in childbirth and relational conflict with her spouse. Next up was the man, who was cursed to toilsome labor for the rest of his days. God then cursed the very ground itself. The world that was meant to continually demonstrate God's greatness would now be twisted and marred by thorns, thistles. and all other sorts of natural disasters.

Finally, in fulfillment of the promise God made in Genesis 2, the first couple was sentenced to death. Since they had been made from the dust, they would now return to the dust when their physical bodies died. That's a lot of judgment packed into one paragraph!

The story of the Fall ends with a vivid image: "The Lord banished [Adam] from the Garden of Eden . . . he drove the man out" (Genesis 3:23–24). The same God who had created man and placed him in the Garden now drove him out of Eden. To grasp the significance of these two verses, we must understand that Eden was not only Adam and Eve's home and the place of God's blessing, but it was also the place where God dwelt. The first couple was driven out of God's presence. He then placed angels at the entrance of the Garden to bar them from ever being able to re-enter again. Apart from God's grace and his offer of salvation, humankind could not have access to him and know him as their God.

This is what sin does: it separates us from God. Sin doesn't make us bad people. Sin makes us (spiritually) dead people! It divides us from the One who created us, who made us in His image, who gave us a mission in the world, and who loves us deeply. Adam and Eve had brought this pain on themselves. They had made the choice to revolt against God's design, plan, and goodness. God, in turn, gave them what they wanted: a life without his authority and care. It's like children who spurn their parents' love and decide to go their own way. Their revolt leads to all sorts of disaster because they stepped outside of their parent's design, plan, and goodness. Whatever harm they receive, they earned. So it was with Adam and Eve's sin.

The apostle Paul would later describe this as God giving people up to the consequences of their actions (see Romans 1:24–28). Sometimes, parents of teenagers have to deal with a particularly rebellious stage in their children's lives by saying, "Well, if that's the choice you want to make, then you are going to have to live with the consequences." Soon, their children are likely to realize the massive amount of things they took for granted!

God does the same with his people. He allows their free will, wrapped in rebellion, to continue to the point that they experience the negative consequences of their actions. While this response may seem harsh, it's actually a supreme act of love. God loves his people so much that he wants them to experience the consequences of life without him so that the resulting pain will cause them to turn from their sins and come back to him. Remember, God ultimately had a plan in place to fix sin through Jesus Christ. So there was, is, and has always been hope for sinners.

5. How does the statement that "sin doesn't make us bad people, it makes us (spiritually) dead people" land on you?

6. Think about a time when you've experienced the consequences of a sin. How did God use those consequences to reveal your ultimate need for him?

REFLECT

The Reality of Physical Death

Adam and Eve's deaths did not come immediately after they sinned. This is another act of grace! God would have been just to judge Adam and Eve's sin by ending their lives on the spot. But he allowed them to live on in spite of their sin. True, they did experience a death on the day they sinned because they were separated from God—they were now dead in their sin. But they did not physically die at that moment—that would come later. Instead of living forever in the presence of God, they were cursed to a temporary life that would end one day.

Both of these punishments are still in force today. All people die physically. Some are taken from this life tragically, with unforeseen illness, suffering, or accidents that end their lives when they are relatively young. Others live to a normative age and die a "natural" death. But in reality, there is no such thing as a natural death. All death, even predictable ones, are unwelcome intruders into the flow of life. Someone is alive one minute and the next they are gone. Physical death is terrible.

7. When is the first time you remember understanding the reality of death? What happened and how did you respond?

8. How do you typically process death—either the prospect of your own or someone you love—at this point in your life?

The Reality of Spiritual Death

The second form of judgment is still intact as well. Sin continues to bring spiritual separation from God because "all have sinned and fall short of the glory of God" (Romans 3:23). When we sin, we are found guilty before God, and the judgment for our sin is the same as given to Adam and Eve: "For the wages of sin is death" (6:23). Death is what we earn when we sin. Just as Adam and Eve were separated from the presence of God, so we are separated from God when we sin. We experience the death of separation in this life, and apart from the gracious intervention of God, we will experience this separation from God in the afterlife.

This is a hard reality for most people. "A loving God would never send people to hell," some might contend. But as we've seen, God *must* judge sin because he is just. Imagine how repulsed we would be if a self-confessed murderer was acquitted for the crimes he committed simply because the judge wanted to show him love. While love is commendable, our visceral reaction would show that we believe something was wrong with that arrangement.

A guilty person should be held accountable for his or her crimes. A judge who decides otherwise is not just and is no longer worthy of the position. The murderer may not welcome a just punishment, but if a law has been broken, the wrongdoing must be punished. The same is true of God's law. If we have broken it, he must keep his word and punish us. He has already told us the punishment will be death, so it shouldn't be a surprise when that happens. Hell is the natural outcome of our revolt. We turn from God and get what our sin deserves.

This fact should awaken us to the reality of God's judgment and press us to turn to him before it's too late. In this life, we may be able to sin, incur judgment, and continue to live, but the day is coming when the sand in the hourglass of life will run out. On that day, there will be no second chances. As the writer of Hebrews states, "People are destined to die once, and after that to face judgment" (9:27). This is the fate that awaits us all.

But thankfully, that doesn't have to be the only outcome! Some 2,000 years ago, Jesus came to this earth and offered himself as a perfect sacrifice for our sins on a Roman cross. When we accept what he has done for us—his payment for our sins—and choose to live for him, we are restored to God and do not have to face the prospect of eternal separation from him. When we come to Christ in faith and repentance, we do not have to fear that final judgment.

9. What kind of separation from God do we experience when we sin?

10. Do you think God has the right to punish sin the way that does? Explain your response.

CLOSE

The good news is that if you're reading this lesson, you are still alive. There is still time for you to turn to God. In fact, the Bible records the story of a man who was saved in the nick of time: a criminal who hung next to Jesus on a cross. The man cried out for mercy and asked Jesus to remember him when He entered into heaven (see Luke 23:42).

Jesus answered with words that drip with hope for all sinners: "Truly I tell you, today you will be with me in paradise" (verse 43). Who knows what kind of life this man might have lived. It definitely wasn't one filled with moral purity and virtue, given that he was being executed for a capital offense. But God was not fazed by the criminal's past. He was willing to forgive the man's sins even in the final hours—perhaps even final minutes—of his life.

This same hope extends to you today. You do not have to face the consequences you deserve for your sins. God has made a way to save sinners and fix the world through Jesus Christ, and you can trust in his plan *now* before you face that final day of judgment.

If you are unsure of your standing before God—if you fear the final judgment because you do not know if your sins have been forgiven—lean in to a relationship with someone you know who claims to be a Christian. Perhaps reach out to someone in a church you've connected with in some way, or someone who lives near you, works with you, or attends the same school as you. Ask that person how you can find forgiveness and hope through Jesus Christ.

If you are a Christian and know that your sins have been forgiven, praise the Lord for showing you his grace and mercy. Just like the criminal on the cross, you have much for which to be thankful. You know that God will remember you in his kingdom.

11. How does the reality of sin impact how you see the world, others, and God's justice?

12. How will this study influence how you live your life from this point on?

Lesson 3

SIN NATURE

The Lᴏʀᴅ said, "What have you done? Listen!
Your brother's blood cries out to me from the ground.
Now you are under a curse and driven from the ground."

GENESIS 4:10–11

Therefore, just as sin entered the world through
one man, and death through sin, and in this way death
came to all people, because all sinned.

ROMANS 5:12

If anyone . . . knows
the good they ought
to do and doesn't do it,
it is sin for them.

— JAMES 4:17

WELCOME

I find it funny that when I run into people who know both me and my father, they will often remark, "You look just like your daddy." Now, I love my dad and view their comment as a high compliment, so I usually respond by simply saying, "Thank you." However, the sarcastic side of me always wants to respond by saying, "Isn't biology amazing?" I mean, who did you think I would look like? (Of course, I never say this, I just think it.)

There is a predictable pattern that occurs almost every time a new child is born. People visit the new parents in the hospital and say something like, "She's got her daddy's nose," or, "Just look at those cheeks—they're just like her mommy's." It's fun to look at a newborn and consider their physical characteristics and think about from whom those distinctive attributes may have come.

Certain physical traits like these may be easy to see—even at birth. But it will take some time for other aspects of what the child has inherited from their parents to come into play. Down the road, someone might attribute the child's hot temper to a trait picked up from their father, or the child's charm and social savvy from their mother. Time will reveal how similar a child's physical and psychological attributes are to each parent. But all children will naturally bear one distinguishing mark: a sin nature.

As we discussed in the previous session, the apostle Paul wrote that "all have sinned and fall short of the glory of God" (Romans 3:23). Most people will intuitively agree with this claim—at least on a surface level. While they may not define sin as an offense against God or as disobedience to his law, most people recognize that we all do bad things from time to time. This reality is compounded if we consider our thoughts, emotions, and motives, as we so often think or feel things that are just not right.

1. What are some of the defining traits (physical and emotional) that you have picked up from your parents?

2. How do you respond to the statement that all children are born with a "sin nature"? Does this seem fair or unfair to you? Explain your response.

READ

A Direct Reflection of Our Parents

As a parent, one of the most frightening realities for me is the fact that my children are a direct reflection of me, for better or worse. Not only do they have my biological attributes, but they also exhibit attributes of my character. This reality is emphasized in our family by the fact that we have two adopted children. Although they do not bear my biological characteristics, they do reflect my behavior—both the good moments and the not-so-good moments.

Scripture reveals that Adam and Eve also passed down some not-so-good traits to their children as a direct result of their sin. "Eve . . . became pregnant and gave birth to Cain. . . . Later she gave birth to his brother Abel" (Genesis 4:1–2). Abel kept flocks, while Cain worked the soil. Both men brought an offering to the Lord—Cain from the fruits of the soil, and Abel from the firstborn of his flock. Here is what happened next:

*² Now Abel kept flocks, and Cain worked the soil. ³ In the course of time Cain brought some of the fruits of the soil as an offering to the L*ORD*. ⁴ And Abel also brought an offering—fat portions from some of the firstborn of his flock. The L*ORD* looked with favor on Abel and his offering, ⁵ but on Cain and his offering he did not look with favor. So Cain was very angry, and his face was downcast.*

*⁶ Then the L*ORD* said to Cain, "Why are you angry? Why is your face downcast? ⁷ If you do what is right, will you not be accepted? But if you do not do what is right, sin is crouching at your door; it desires to have you, but you must rule over it."*

⁸ Now Cain said to his brother Abel, "Let's go out to the field." While they were in the field, Cain attacked his brother Abel and killed him.

*⁹ Then the L*ORD* said to Cain, "Where is your brother Abel?"*

"I don't know," he replied. "Am I my brother's keeper?"

*¹⁰ The L*ORD* said, "What have you done? Listen! Your brother's blood cries out to me from the ground. ¹¹ Now you are under a curse and driven from the ground, which opened its mouth to receive your brother's blood from your hand. ¹² When you work the ground, it will no longer yield its crops for you. You will be a restless wanderer on the earth."*

Genesis 4:2–12

3. What does the story of Cain reveal about our own sin nature?

4. What similarities do you see between Cain's response when God called him out on his sin and Adam and Eve's response when God called out their sin?

The Cause of Our Sin Nature

Although we might conclude that Cain's sin of murder was far worse than his parents' little bite of forbidden fruit, the Bible actually makes a more startling point: Cain's sin of murder was initiated by Adam and Eve's revolt. Paul writes, "Just as sin entered the world through one man, and death through sin . . . death came to all people, because all sinned" (Romans 5:12). Let's work through the claims of this passage in reverse order.

First, Paul writes that all people have sinned. People think, feel, and do evil things. The Bible defines this as disobedience to God and His word. Second, because all have sinned, death spread to all people, because the wages of sin is death. Death—including physical death in this life and spiritual separation from God—is the natural outcome of a life of sin. This is what sinners deserve for their actions. God is holy and just, so he cannot allow sinful people to remain in a relationship with Him. He cannot let their sin go unpunished.

Finally, this sin, leading to death, is the result of the sin of one man (Adam) in the Garden so long ago. It's that final claim that is most important for our consideration in this lesson, because this truth shapes almost everything else that happens in God's story.

5. What does the Bible say is the source of our sin nature?

6. How have you seen the impact of our sin nature in the world around you?

Our True Condition

All sin is the result of Adam's sin. You might read that as if all men and women follow Adam's example of sin. Using that logic, history is one long chain of evil that is caused by every generation's modeling the failures of the previous one. Cain watched his parents sin and followed suit, and then his children watched his sin and adopted his evil actions for themselves. Each passing generation exhibited the same pattern of sin that they picked up by watching those who had come before them.

While it is certainly true that people follow the example of others and sin as a result, the Bible actually makes a far stronger claim. According to Ecclesiastes 7:20, "There is no one on earth who is righteous, no one who does what is right and never sins." In Psalm 51:5, we read that we are all "sinful at birth, sinful from the time [we are] conceived." The apostle Paul adds, "Through the disobedience of the one man the many were made sinners" (Romans 5:19).

Paul states that people were "made sinners" because of Adam's sin. People did not merely follow Adam's example in doing sin—they actually inherited a sin nature and the consequences that followed his sinful choice. Since Adam is the head of the entire human race, everyone who was born after him inherited his sinful identity.

This is why the Bible says that people are born sinful. Even before they sin, they are already sinners, simply because they are people, and all people are sinners. Dogs are dogs, elephants are elephants, and people are sinners. Sin is their default state of being. It's who they are, and as a result of their sinful nature, they do sinful actions. Or, said another way, all people are sinners (their identity) who sin (their actions).

Our actions naturally follow our identity. Not the other way around.

Think about this contrast in the life of a professional basketball player. On draft day, he is chosen by a team and signs a contract. In that moment, his identity changes. He is now a professional basketball player, and he begins to act according to that new identity. He receives a team jersey, shows up at practice, forms relationships with his teammates, learns the offensive and defensive strategies, and tries to improve his skill to make the team better.

Now imagine a super fan who attempts to complete the same actions without the identity. He would be arrested in short order if he just showed up at practice and started warming up with the team. He can't participate in the team's layup drill or wear the jersey because he's not a professional basketball player. His actions are not in line with his identity.

This order—actions following identity—is the way the world is designed. This means the claim of the Bible is far harsher than you might otherwise assume. The Bible does not merely say that humanity's problem is our sinful actions. If this were the case, then the Bible's solution could be as simple as "stop sinning!" But it's not that simple. The Bible says that we are sinners.

7. According to Psalm 51:5, when did sin enter into our lives?

8. According to Romans 5:19, why is it impossible for us to escape our sin nature?

REFLECT

Paul said this about those who have not been saved by grace through faith in Jesus Christ: "You were dead in your transgressions and sins, in which you used to live when you followed the ways of this world and of the ruler of the kingdom of the air, the spirit who is now at work in those who are disobedient. All of us also lived among them at one time, gratifying the cravings of our flesh and following its desires and thoughts. Like the rest, we were by nature deserving of wrath" (Ephesians 2:1–3).

Did you catch it? Paul did not say that some people were dead in their trespasses and sins, but that all people were in that state. None of us had to commit sin to become a sinner. We merely had to be born. Which means that every cute baby is born dead in trespasses and sins. This might seem harsh, but ask anyone who has been a parent for more than a few months, and they will quickly attest to this reality. All people are sinful from birth.

And what do sinners do? They commit sinful actions. Like Paul says, they follow Satan, indulge their passions, and do whatever their bodies and minds want to do. Of course, no two people are going to sin in exactly the same ways, but all people work out their sinful identity in actions that deviate from God's design, plan, and goodness—just like their first parents, Adam and Eve. People do sinful things because they are sinners.

Paul says that those who are dead in their sins are children of God's wrath. In a very real way, all people are children of God. They are products of his creative handiwork, whether they acknowledge him as their Father or not. But because of the sinful identity they inherited from Adam and Eve, their relationship with God has shifted, and they are now children of his wrath—just like everyone else with a sinful identity. Left to their own devices, they will experience God's wrath, both in this life and the next.

Remember the scene at the end of Genesis 3, when God kicked Adam and Eve out of the Garden of Eden and barred them from reentering. Try as they might, the first couple could not make their way back into God's presence again on their own. In the same way, people who are dead in their trespasses and sins also cannot make themselves come alive.

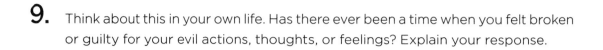

9. Think about this in your own life. Has there ever been a time when you felt broken or guilty for your evil actions, thoughts, or feelings? Explain your response.

10. What did you try to do at that time as a result of those feelings?

CLOSE

It's common for people to experience feelings of shame and guilt for their wrong choices, even if they don't attribute those choices to sinful actions or conviction from God. They might say something like, "I hit rock bottom," or "I just couldn't go on anymore," or even "I just wanted to give up." These exasperated expressions give voice to the hopelessness and helplessness of our sinful identity. We have an intuitive sense that we can't live up to our lofty expectations of ourselves, much less those of God.

Unfortunately, most people who experience an awareness of how messed up they actually are believe the answer is to try to work, or earn, their way back to God. To use the image of the Garden, they to try to walk the path to get back to Eden. But they soon find that, try as they might, they cannot make their way back to God any more than Adam and Eve could.

So . . . is there any hope for us? The Bible's answer is a resounding yes! There is hope, not because people can find their way back to God, but because God came looking for his people. Starting right after the Fall, the Bible tells the story of God's leaving the Garden in relentless pursuit of sinners like you and me. While we can't make our own way back to him, he can find us—just like he found Adam and Eve hiding behind a bush in the Garden on that fateful day so long ago. The only hope for sinners is for God to do something to change their identity—which is exactly what he does through Jesus Christ.

11. What does the impact of sin in this world tell us about our need for a Savior?

12. How do you respond to this fact that *God* is the one who seeks out sinners?

Lesson 4

COMPLETELY BROKEN

*"Come, let us build ourselves a city, with a tower
that reaches to the heavens, so that we may make a name
for ourselves; otherwise we will be scattered over the
face of the whole earth."*

GENESIS 11:4

*But whoever looks intently into the perfect law
that gives freedom, and continues in it—not forgetting
what they have heard, but doing it—they will be
blessed in what they do.*

JAMES 1:25

Stand firm . . . and do not let yourselves be burdened again by a yoke of slavery.

— GALATIANS 5:1

WELCOME

Breaking news. If you open up a news site on your phone right now, you will immediately find a story that draws your attention, or at least your curiosity. Whether it's
about a movie star, politician, or athlete, someone famous has made headlines for
doing something foolish. The frequency of fake news does little to undermine the
legitimate accusations of wrongdoing and scandal.

What's fascinating is how deep that rabbit hole often goes. The first story hints at
the dirty details, and then, as the days pass, more and more information comes to
light. A minor public relations issue becomes a national scandal, leading to someone
being fired or resigning and their image forever linked to their impropriety.

Pay attention to this cycle, and you'll eventually ask the question, "How deep is this
one going to go?" We begin to just assume that more information will eventually
come out, more firsthand accounts will surface, more pictures and more secret emails
will come to light. Things always seem to get far worse before they get better.

1. Think of a situation where what was initially reported in the news was just the
beginning of the story. What eventually came out in that situation?

2. Do you think it is always the case that there is always "more to the story" when it comes to our sin nature? Explain your response.

READ

The Curse Still in Effect

The story of humanity, as told in the Bible, also causes us to ask, "How deep does the rabbit hole of sin actually go?" In the account of Adam and Eve, we are immediately clued in to the fact that things are going to get much worse for them and their descendants. As we saw in the last lesson, immediately after Adam and Eve are kicked out of the Garden, one of their children kills another in a fit of jealousy (see Genesis 4). We're barely two pages into the Bible by this point and we've already got murder plaguing creation. Here is what we read next:

[1] *This is the written account of Adam's family line.*

When God created mankind, he made them in the likeness of God. [2] *He created them male and female and blessed them. And he named them "Mankind" when they were created.*

³ *When Adam had lived 130 years, he had a son in his own likeness, in his own image; and he named him Seth.* ⁴ *After Seth was born, Adam lived 800 years and had other sons and daughters.* ⁵ *Altogether, Adam lived a total of 930 years, and then he died.*

⁶ *When Seth had lived 105 years, he became the father of Enosh.* ⁷ *After he became the father of Enosh, Seth lived 807 years and had other sons and daughters.* ⁸ *Altogether, Seth lived a total of 912 years, and then he died.*

⁹ *When Enosh had lived 90 years, he became the father of Kenan.* ¹⁰ *After he became the father of Kenan, Enosh lived 815 years and had other sons and daughters.* ¹¹ *Altogether, Enosh lived a total of 905 years, and then he died.*

¹² *When Kenan had lived 70 years, he became the father of Mahalalel.* ¹³ *After he became the father of Mahalalel, Kenan lived 840 years and had other sons and daughters.* ¹⁴ *Altogether, Kenan lived a total of 910 years, and then he died.*

¹⁵ *When Mahalalel had lived 65 years, he became the father of Jared.* ¹⁶ *After he became the father of Jared, Mahalalel lived 830 years and had other sons and daughters.* ¹⁷ *Altogether, Mahalalel lived a total of 895 years, and then he died.*

¹⁸ *When Jared had lived 162 years, he became the father of Enoch.* ¹⁹ *After he became the father of Enoch, Jared lived 800 years and had other sons and daughters.* ²⁰ *Altogether, Jared lived a total of 962 years, and then he died.*

²¹ *When Enoch had lived 65 years, he became the father of Methuselah.* ²² *After he became the father of Methuselah, Enoch walked faithfully with God 300 years and had other sons and daughters.* ²³ *Altogether, Enoch lived a total of 365 years.* ²⁴ *Enoch walked faithfully with God; then he was no more, because God took him away.*

²⁵ *When Methuselah had lived 187 years, he became the father of Lamech.* ²⁶ *After he became the father of Lamech, Methuselah lived 782 years and had other sons and daughters.* ²⁷ *Altogether, Methuselah lived a total of 969 years, and then he died.*

²⁸ When Lamech had lived 182 years, he had a son. ²⁹ He named him Noah and said, "He will comfort us in the labor and painful toil of our hands caused by the ground the Lᴏʀᴅ has cursed." ³⁰ After Noah was born, Lamech lived 595 years and had other sons and daughters. ³¹ Altogether, Lamech lived a total of 777 years, and then he died.

³² After Noah was 500 years old, he became the father of Shem, Ham and Japheth.

Genesis 5:1–32

It might be easy to just gloss over this portion of Scripture, but the repetition of the phrase "and then he died" reminds us that the original curse is still in effect. Although each of Adam's descendants lived for many years, eventually they all died. Death is a metronome that constantly beats in the background of human existence.

3. What does the author of this passage remind us about in verses 1–2? Why do you think the writer added this detail?

4. Notice the statement made about Noah in verse 29. What is the author reminding us about here again at the end of this genealogy?

The Cycle Continues

What follows next in Genesis 6 describes a cryptic scene of sexual deviance that leads God to conclude, "I regret that I have made them" (verse 7). This is a far cry from God's verdict in the Garden, where he described his creation, particularly men and women, as "very good" (1:31).

God's anger with human sin results in judgment—this time with a flood that destroys much of his creation. The severity of this response reveals the disgusting nature of sin and how far-reaching the perversion had become. Yet God, in his grace, still chose to spare Noah, his family, and a pair of each living thing that he had made (see Genesis 7–9). This reveals, once more, that God has not abandoned his people forever and is still at work to save them.

Genesis 10 contains another genealogical list of the people who came after Noah—the descendants of his sons Shem, Ham, and Japheth. We are told, "From these [three sons] the nations spread out over the earth after the flood" (verse 32). When we come to Genesis 11, we find that humanity once again has decided to delve deep into sin, even after experiencing God's judgment through the flood. This time it is through the construction of a tower:

> ¹¹ *Now the whole world had one language and a common speech.* ² *As people moved eastward, they found a plain in Shinar and settled there.*

³ They said to each other, "Come, let's make bricks and bake them thoroughly." They used brick instead of stone, and tar for mortar. ⁴ Then they said, "Come, let us build ourselves a city, with a tower that reaches to the heavens, so that we may make a name for ourselves; otherwise we will be scattered over the face of the whole earth."

*⁵ But the L*ORD *came down to see the city and the tower the people were building. ⁶ The L*ORD *said, "If as one people speaking the same language they have begun to do this, then nothing they plan to do will be impossible for them. ⁷ Come, let us go down and confuse their language so they will not understand each other."*

*⁸ So the L*ORD *scattered them from there over all the earth, and they stopped building the city. ⁹ That is why it was called Babel—because there the L*ORD *confused the language of the whole world. From there the L*ORD *scattered them over the face of the whole earth.*

Genesis 11:1–9

If you were watching this story as a movie, you might be tempted to conclude the plot is boring and walk right out of the theater. Every episode seems to be a repeat performance of the way the story started. Although the details are different, Babel and the Garden are one and the same in many ways. In both episodes, people were unwilling to submit to God's rule and revolted against his authority. Both did what they wanted regardless of the consequences. Both elevated themselves in pride. And, in both stories, God judged them.

Notice that God's judgment in Genesis 11 follows a similar pattern. The people were attempting to build a tower to heaven so they could make a name for themselves—yet God "came down to see the city and the tower the people were building" (verse 5). It's like a toddler calling his dad over to see his towering stack of Legos. "Come here, daddy! Look at this really, really, big tower I've made!" The dad then kneels down to take a look at the imposing, six-inch stack of blocks that barely rises to his ankles.

But in this example, the dad would be impressed by his son's effort. Not so with God. Not only is the Lord unimpressed by the people's tower, but he is also angry. He knows it's a physical manifestation of his people's spiritual revolt. They want to be their own gods instead of submitting to him as God. What God does next is exactly what their sin deserves. He scatters the people and confuses their language to make it impossible (or at least difficult) to ever unite in revolt this way again. God's people are a long way from Eden, both physically and spiritually.

5. What reason did the people give for wanting to build a tower?

6. What do you think was the impact on humanity when God scattered the people?

REFLECT

We All Are Completely Broken

This raises an important question for us today: How should we see ourselves in the story of the Tower of Babel? The way we seek to answer this question reveals an important truth about the way in which the Bible is meant to be used. James, a New Testament writer, challenges us to use the Bible the way we would use a mirror (see James 1:22–25). We use a mirror because it reveals things about us that are out of whack and need to be adjusted.

We don't look in a mirror, notice a big chunk of lettuce between our teeth, and walk away without digging it out. If we did, it would defeat the purpose of the mirror. We use a mirror to help us both see and correct problems. The Bible is meant to be used in the same way—as a mirror that helps us see our sin for what it is. The reason the story in the Garden or the episode at Babel resonates with us is because it is so easy for us to read ourselves into those stories. In thousands of years of human history, we still sin in much the same way.

Why is this the case? The reason is because we are completely broken. Now, this doesn't mean everything about us is broken. There are certainly aspects of beauty, good, joy, and hope found in all people, and humanity is not as bad as it could be all of the time. Even the most notorious sinner reflects the virtues of love and peace at times. But because of the sin nature we inherited from our first father, Adam, we are all broken.

Let's consider two aspects of that claim. First, the sin nature that we inherited from Adam involves "all" of us. Notice what the following passages say about this:

17 As Jesus started on his way, a man ran up to him and fell on his knees before him. "Good teacher," he asked, "what must I do to inherit eternal life?" 18 "Why do you call me good?" Jesus answered. "No one is good—except God alone.

Mark 10:17–18

10 As it is written: "There is no one righteous, not even one; 11 there is no one who understands; there is no one who seeks God."

Romans 3:10–11

8 If we claim to be without sin, we deceive ourselves and the truth is not in us. 9 If we confess our sins, he is faithful and just and will forgive us our sins and purify us from all unrighteousness. 10 If we claim we have not sinned, we make him out to be a liar and his word is not in us.

1 John 1:8–10

The clear conviction of the biblical authors is that all people sin. No one escapes sin's grip. Sin is a defining mark for us all. The vast array of physical characteristics that differentiate one person from the next does not mask the unity we all share because of our sin nature.

Next, let's look at the fact that *the* sin nature we inherited from Adam has left all of us "broken." This means that every aspect of who we are is broken. Notice these passages and what they say about the different aspects of a person who is marred by sin:

[21] *"For it is from within, out of a person's heart, that evil thoughts come—sexual immorality, theft, murder,* [22] *adultery, greed, malice, deceit, lewdness, envy, slander, arrogance and folly.* [23] *All these evils come from inside and defile a person."*

Mark 7:21-23

At one time we too were foolish, disobedient, deceived and enslaved by all kinds of passions and pleasures. We lived in malice and envy, being hated and hating one another.

Titus 3:3

[15] *I do not understand what I do. For what I want to do I do not do, but what I hate I do.* [16] *And if I do what I do not want to do, I agree that the law is good.* [17] *As it is, it is no longer I myself who do it, but it is sin living in me.* [18] *For I know that good itself does not dwell in me, that is, in my sinful nature.*

Romans 7:15-18

7. What patterns of sin have you witnessed in the generational history of your family?

8. Notice what Paul writes in Romans 7:15–18. How can you relate to his statement? When have you felt the same way about your sin nature?

Completely Distorted by the Fall

The Bible uses a number of terms to refer to the totality of what makes up a person. It's clear that our actions are broken—we say and do things that are evil. But the rabbit hole goes even deeper. Our minds are also broken—they are twisted and distorted to think wrong thoughts about God and his world. We call evil good and good evil because our minds are warped by sin.

Going even deeper, our will is held captive by sin. Even when we want to do what is right, we fail to live up to our aspirations and spiral right back into the pit once more. Most of us have experienced the frustration of trying to stop doing something we know is wrong. For example, we might recognize that anxiety is crippling us. We can clearly see that our constant worry is harming our relationships. It is leading our closest friends to want to avoid being around us because we are shrouded in constant negativity.

We want to break free and change. We know that our actions and attitudes are destructive to us and those around us. We might not even call that action sin, but we understand that it's hurting us and we want to change. But we are unable to do so because we are held in the grip of sin. Even our hearts are held in its grip. The very core of all people is sinful, and with it our feelings and emotions are volatile and deceptive.

It's a deep rabbit hole indeed. Every aspect of who we are has been broken, twisted, and distorted by the Fall. Jesus used a vivid image to describe our relationship with sin when he said, "Everyone who sins is a slave to sin" (John 8:34). Paul followed suit, noting that people are slaves to whatever they obey (see Romans 6:15–23). Since people obey their sin nature, they are slaves to that sin. Slavery is an apt picture for humans under sin's control because the grip of sin is so total and complete.

9. Have you ever felt like you were a slave to your sin? Give some examples from your life.

10. Have you ever tried to stop a bad habit like worrying? What happened as a result?

CLOSE

Most of us who have tried to make changes to our lives come to the conclusion that we are terrible failures. We might see some momentary wins, like the kind you experience in the first few days or weeks of a new diet, but then reality sets in. We find ourselves right back in the same position once again. We feel trapped . . . because we are!

This is one of the reasons the Bible goes into detail about the Israelites' time spent in slavery to foreign nations. The people God had created to live in submission to him and his word staged a revolt against his authority and—by the start of the second book of the Bible (Exodus)—had found themselves enslaved in Egypt. They were trapped, just like we are in our sin today.

There was no hope for the people's escape unless God delivered them—just as there is no hope for us to escape from sin's clutches unless God does something to deliver us. In the story of the Israelites, God eventually raised up a man named Moses to miraculously lead his people out of slavery in Egypt. In our story, God ultimately sent his only Son, Jesus Christ, into this world to miraculously lead us out of our slavery to sin.

Of course, it isn't fun to think of ourselves this way. We want to be strong and powerful. We long for others to believe we have it all together—that we're competent and capable of doing whatever we want and that nothing can stop us from reaching our full potential. It sounds much better to blame political policy, socio-economic realities, or psychology maladies for the evil we do and experience. It's much easier to point fingers at others than it is to own our sin nature. But we know that it's all a lie. Our lives display that we are completely broken and utterly helpless apart from God's grace. We just have to be willing to admit it.

11. Which of the following statements best reflects your current awareness of your brokenness?

   A. I know that I am hopeless without God freeing me from slavery to sin, and I admit this need to him on a regular basis.

B. There have been times when I've acknowledged my sin and my need for God's deliverance, but on most days, I don't depend on him and admit my need.

C. I feel trapped in my sin, but I don't actually believe God can help me.

D. I'm content with my life as it is and don't see any need for God's help.

12. Are you willing to admit your sin and and your need for grace to another person in your church or community? If so, write down who you will talk to and when. What would be the benefits of doing so?

SYSTEMS OF EVIL

When Moses approached the camp and saw the calf and the dancing, his anger burned and he threw the tablets out of his hands, breaking them to pieces at the foot of the mountain.

E X O D U S   3 2 : 1 9

As for you, you were dead in your transgressions and sins, in which you used to live when you followed the ways of this world and of the ruler of the kingdom of the air, the spirit who is now at work in those who are disobedient.

E P H E S I A N S   2 : 1 – 2

The kings of the
earth rise up . . .
against the Lord and
against his anointed.

— PSALM 2:2

WELCOME

My wife and I have four children. As I write this, three of them are teenagers. I have learned from experience there is nothing that will make a teenager roll his or her eyes faster than one of those notorious parenting quips like, "If all of your friends jumped off a bridge, would you jump too?" And nothing will start an argument faster than a parent telling a child who to (or not to) hang out with or date.

More often than not, parents are onto something with their warnings. They know the people their children spend time with will influence who they become. One rotten apple can spoil the whole bunch. Of course, it's typical for teenagers to ignore these warnings and run headlong into unhealthy relationships. The results are predictable. Friends who lead them to unwise decisions and rebellion. Dating relationships that end in devastation. An unending cycle of momentary thrills followed by despair.

We all like to think we're the exception to this rule. We like to believe we can somehow choose our friends without considering their virtues (or lack thereof) and without causing ourselves the kind of pain we've seen in so many other people's lives. But we're not the exception to the rule. The sin that so easily entangles our lives only intensifies when it is coupled with the sin of those we invite into our inner circle.

Like every other truth in life, this reality is explained in the Bible. Going back to the Garden of Eden, the issue was not merely that an isolated individual sinned, but rather, *two* people sinned together. After picking and eating the fruit, "[Eve] gave some to her husband, who was with her, and he ate it" (Genesis 3:6). Adam wasn't off minding his own business when Eve sauntered up with some fruit. No, Adam was with her. In fact, he was the one whom God had told not to eat the fruit in the first place (see 2:16–17).

Eve did not cause Adam to sin. But they did sin together.

1. What impact do you think it had that Adam and Eve were together when they chose to disobey God and eat from the forbidden tree?

2. Why are people more likely to be influenced to engage in sin when they are with others? How can a group fan the fires of each person's sin?

READ

Trading Real for Fake

Throughout the Old Testament, we see account after account of the Israelites vacillating from trusting God to worshiping idols. After God raised up Moses to lead the Israelites out of slavery in Egypt, he led the people through the Red Sea—which God miraculously parted for them—and into the wilderness (see Exodus 14–18). After a brief journey, the people arrived at the foot of Mount Sinai, where the Lord "called Moses to the top of the mountain" (19:20).

It was there that God gave Moses the Ten Commandments and other laws and instructions on how the Israelites were to live as his people. But even before Moses came down from the mountain, the people lost their faith in God. They forgot about all the things that he had done to bring them out of slavery in Egypt and provide for their needs (in the form of manna, quail, and water) in the desert. Here is what happened in their story:

[1] *When the people saw that Moses was so long in coming down from the mountain, they gathered around Aaron and said, "Come, make us gods who will go before us. As for this fellow Moses who brought us up out of Egypt, we don't know what has happened to him."*

[2] *Aaron answered them, "Take off the gold earrings that your wives, your sons and your daughters are wearing, and bring them to me."* [3] *So all the people took off their earrings and brought them to Aaron.* [4] *He took what they handed him and made it into an idol cast in the shape of a calf, fashioning it with a tool. Then they said, "These are your gods, Israel, who brought you up out of Egypt." . . .*

[19] *When Moses approached the camp and saw the calf and the dancing, his anger burned and he threw the tablets out of his hands, breaking them to pieces at the foot of the mountain.* [20] *And he took the calf the people had made and burned it in the fire; then he ground it to powder, scattered it on the water and made the Israelites drink it.*

[21] *He said to Aaron, "What did these people do to you, that you led them into such great sin?"*

[22] *"Do not be angry, my lord," Aaron answered. "You know how prone these people are to evil.* [23] *They said to me, 'Make us gods who will go before us. As for this fellow Moses who brought us up out of Egypt, we don't know what has happened to him.'* [24] *So I told them, 'Whoever has any gold jewelry, take it off.' Then they gave me the gold, and I threw it into the fire, and out came this calf!"*

[25] *Moses saw that the people were running wild and that Aaron had let them get out of control and so become a laughingstock to their enemies.* [26] *So he stood at the entrance to the camp and said, "Whoever is for the LORD, come to me." And all the Levites rallied to him.*

[27] *Then he said to them, "This is what the LORD, the God of Israel, says: 'Each man strap a sword to his side. Go back and forth through the camp from one end to the other, each killing his brother and friend and neighbor.'"* [28] *The Levites*

did as Moses commanded, and that day about three thousand of the people died. ²⁹ *Then Moses said, "You have been set apart to the LORD today, for you were against your own sons and brothers, and he has blessed you this day."*

³⁰ *The next day Moses said to the people, "You have committed a great sin. But now I will go up to the LORD; perhaps I can make atonement for your sin."*

Exodus 32:1–4, 19–30

This incident with the golden calf is just one of many examples of the Israelites turning from the worship of the one true God to the worship of false idols. It happened here, as recorded in this account from Exodus. It happened after the people conquered the Promised Land and began to be influenced by their neighbors, as recorded in the book of Judges. It happened after the people were given a king, became united under David, and then split into the kingdoms of Israel and Judah, as recorded in the books of 1 and 2 Samuel through 1 and 2 Kings. Time and again, the people forgot God's goodness and shifted their allegiances to fake gods.

3. Why do you think the Israelites turned to worshiping a god made by their own hands after witnessing all the miraculous things that God had done?

4. What role does remembering God's faithfulness play in trusting God for the future?

The Power of Groups

We tend to think of idolatry as something that took place in ancient times. But the worship of idols is very much alive today. Just consider a false god like fame. People worship fame every day! They choose jobs based on what best positions them for public praise. They make significant decisions in light of what will make them seem more important or powerful to others. Notice those last two words: "to others." The god of fame can't exist without others around to call the person famous. The only way fame can be appealing is when others are there to notice.

Or think about the false god of money. People certainly worship money in our day! Our culture promotes the false belief that money will buy us whatever we want—including happiness—and allow us to spend our days in ease and luxury. But again, who wants to do that alone? Most of us would become bored after a short time of private indulgence. Most of us want other people to enjoy our money—or the things we buy with our money—with us.

The group doesn't make the revolt worse. Sin is always offensive to a holy God. But groups do make the consequences of sin in this life more prominent and severe.

One clear example of where "the group" magnifies the consequences of sin is racism. Racism is, at its core, an individual evil. It undermines the reality that all people, regardless of their skin color, are created in the image of God and have intrinsic worth and value. We are all responsible for our own failure to love our brothers and sisters as we should. When we fail to love others as God has loved us, it reveals that we don't truly understand or appreciate the gospel of Jesus Christ, who willingly came to this earth, took on the form of a servant, and died a criminal's death for people who were not like him (see Philippians 2:1–11).

But the sin of racism picks up steam when it infects an entire culture. History shows us that groups align in this sin, working out the implications of their false view of humanity with all sorts of heinous evil. The hatred that fueled the first murder between Cain and Abel now takes root in entire cultures. People born into such cultures have a tendency to pick up on the negative patterns of thought and behavior that they see in those they interact with every day.

Sexual sin is another example. Left alone, we're all guilty of our fair share of perverted thoughts and practices. We can see from the Bible (and subsequent human history) that sexual deviance has always been a primary way for people to rebel against God. But what happens when sexual sin takes root in a group? The power of the group makes the reality of evil even worse.

5. What are some of the false gods in our day that are easier to worship in a group?

6. What is an example of a personal sin that has even worse consequences when it is encouraged to be practiced by a group?

REFLECT

Choosing Our Friends Wisely

As we saw in the previous lesson, we are all born dead in our sins and can't help but do bad things as a result. We are sinners who sin! And now, we see that we are sinners who sin with *other* sinners. The combination of our sin creates systems of evil that are built into the fabric of society. The apostle Paul tells us that apart from the grace of God, all of us embrace these systems of evil because we are following "the ways of this world and of the ruler of the kingdom of the air, the spirit who is now at work in those who are disobedient" (Ephesians 2:2). We're modeling the sin of Adam and Eve and enacting our revolt against God.

Perhaps it is for this reason that the Bible warns us to choose our friends wisely and resist the pull of our world, as the following passages relate:

Blessed is the one who does not walk in step with the wicked or stand in the way that sinners take or sit in the company of mockers.

Psalm 1:1

Walk with the wise and become wise, for a companion of fools suffers harm.

Proverbs 13:20

A friend loves at all times, and a brother is born for a time of adversity.

Proverbs 17:17

One who has unreliable friends soon comes to ruin, but there is a friend who sticks closer than a brother.

Proverbs 18:24

Do not be yoked together with unbelievers. For what do righteousness and wickedness have in common? Or what fellowship can light have with darkness?

2 Corinthians 6:14

Because of our slavery to sin, we do not obey the wisdom of these passages. We are trapped and, given enough time, we will all cave in and form relationships that further entrench our sin nature. As nice as it would be to be able to simply recognize the power of group sin and avoid it, we can't. Unless God intervenes, we are trapped.

7. In what ways do other people tend to influence your thoughts, feelings, and actions?

8. What do these passages say about the importance of choosing the right friends?

The Role of the Church

The nation of Israel experienced their slavery to sin time and time again. The Israelites were meant to worship God as a group. He was, after all, their God, and they were his people (see Exodus 6:7). Their defining mark as a nation was meant to be the fact that God dwelt among them. He had saved them by his grace, sustained them with his love, and taught them through his law. They had every opportunity to be a group that got it right.

But they didn't. In many ways, the story of the Israelites in the Old Testament is the story of a national failure—on repeat. Although the characters and stories change, the people in the tale consistently prove they are incapable of keeping God's law and walking faithfully with him. Rather than living as a distinct people, they continue to worship the false gods of the surrounding nations. So God raised up a series of prophets whose writings and teachings reminded the Israelites that God would judge them for their revolt (as recorded in the books of Isaiah through Malachi). The entire nation faced the punishment its united sin deserved.

The same fate awaits those who live in blatant disregard for God today. They are judged for living in outright revolt to God's design and for encouraging others to do the same. Their guilt and condemnation are clear—and God's judgment is just.

Only those who have been saved by God's grace and experienced his mercy are capable of escaping the power of systemic sin. Jesus' work and the Holy Spirit's power make it possible for us to walk in love toward others and resist the pattern of sin that has been set by this world. We have been called to stand against all forms of social evil and fight on behalf of everyone made in God's image. The local church is called to be a countercultural community intent on loving people who are ensnared in sin and, at the same time, working to oppose sin in all its forms.

9. How does Jesus' work and the power of the Holy Spirit enable Christians to fight against the evil patterns of sin in our world?

10. How should Christians today be involved in bringing God's grace to the sins that plague our culture and our world?

CLOSE

The local church is the most magnificent force for good in this world. Together, those who have been saved by God's grace can have a massive impact both in their local communities and around the globe. I would like to encourage you to find time this week to chat with a few people who know and love Jesus. Ask how God has used them to bring hope and healing to the world. Before you begin the next lesson, spend a few minutes praying about what role you might play in helping others see that Jesus can break the power of sin—even the sins of entire cultures.

11. What is the power of a group when it comes to countering systems of evil in this world? How have you seen that play out?

12. What happens if you try to grow in godliness on your own? What are some ways that the church and your fellow Christians have helped you to mature in your faith?

GLIMMERS OF HOPE

But he was pierced for our transgressions, he was crushed for our iniquities; the punishment that brought us peace was on him, and by his wounds we are healed.

ISAIAH 53:5

For this reason Christ is the mediator of a new covenant, that those who are called may receive the promised eternal inheritance—now that he has died as a ransom to set them free from the sins committed under the first covenant.

HEBREWS 9:15

From the LORD

comes deliverance.

May your blessing

be on your people.

— PSALM 3:8

WELCOME

On September 12, 1962, President John F. Kennedy stood on a platform in Rice University Stadium and cast a vision to send a man to the moon. Up until this point, the dream of sending a human into outer space was inconceivable. Truth be told, the odds seemed to not favor the possibility that a human could survive such a mission. However, President Kennedy provided something that day—he provided hope. His passion, backed by a firm belief in American ingenuity, was enough to ultimately catapult the space program to the moon.

As you get ready to dive into this last lesson, you should be asking one question: Is there any hope? We have seen that Adam and Eve's wrongdoing birthed into humanity the sin that would infest the human soul and shape every culture. The outworking of everything evil in this world can be attributed to that fateful day in the Garden so long ago. Things certainly seemed hopeless.

There's nothing worse than an overwhelming feeling of hopelessness. You've probably been there at some point in your life—hours, days, or weeks when you felt like the world was crashing in and there was nothing you could do to make it stop. You will understand that "hope deferred makes the heart sick" (Proverbs 13:12). Sometimes this feeling simply won't go away and even plagues you for years.

There's no way to fully describe the feeling of utter hopelessness unless you've actually lived through it. Others want to understand, and they express concern, but they can't really get inside your mind or do much to make things any better. The mother who just miscarried or the dad who lost his job may be able to put on a smiling face and navigate their responsibilities, but in quiet moments of reflection, hopelessness cripples them and makes it hard for them to press forward. Hopelessness seems to have a mind of its own.

If the events of the Fall represented the whole of our story, we would be left with a sense of despair that would make our earthly angst all the more crushing. The truth that we have been considering throughout this study is that we were born enslaved to sin and there is nothing we can do in our strength to help us escape the death-grip of this dastardly foe. To make matters worse, sin plagues all people, locking the world in systems of entrenched sin that bring grave harm on those who are made in God's image. As a result, all men and women stand before God guilty of sin and deserving of death as a just punishment for their revolt.

This is bad news indeed.

But it's not the only news! The Bible is actually a book of *good* news from cover to cover. In fact, that is what the word *gospel* means—the good news of Jesus Christ's work to save sinners and fix the world. Unfortunately, many people don't know how to get from the early chapters of Genesis to Jesus. They may have heard that Jesus is at the heart of Christianity and the core of the Bible's message, but they are unsure as to how this actually works. As a result of this disconnection, many people today miss out on the beautiful ways the Bible points us to Christ. He is all over the Bible . . . even way back in the opening chapters of Genesis.

1. Have you ever felt hopeless? What do you do as a result of that feeling?

2. What does God promise in Genesis 3:15? How do you see Jesus in the first three chapters to Genesis? How do you see him in the Old Testament?

READ

God's Plan to Defeat Satan

Perhaps you find it difficult to believe that Jesus was present even back in the early chapters of Genesis. But in Genesis 3:15, when God was issuing the curse against humanity, we read of his plan to send Jesus into the world to save people from sin: "I will put enmity between you [Satan] and the woman, and between your offspring and hers; he will crush your head, and you will strike his heel." It is amazing news! Not only does God curse the serpent, but he also promises that a child (or "seed") of Eve will be born who will crush Satan's head and permanently defeat him, sin, and death. The name of this child is not yet known, but it is clear that he will right the wrongs that Adam's sin brought into the world.

The rest of the Old Testament story invites us to ask, "Who is that promised one?" The book of Genesis follows the line of numerous barren women, reminding us that we should be on the lookout for a miraculous child. Is it Abraham? No. He is the father of many nations, but he is not the promised child. Is it Moses? No. He leads the people out of slavery in Egypt, but he certainly doesn't address the sin problem of that people. In fact, he's just as sinful as they are.

Perhaps it is David? He was a man of destiny. Even though he was an unlikely candidate for kingship over Israel, he was personally chosen for the role by God. The Bible even declares that he was "a man after [God's] own heart" (1 Samuel 13:14). David seems the most likely person to inherit these promises. But as the story of his life unfolds, we see that he had a damaging flaw: he was a human being with a sin nature. He was lured away by the lust of his flesh when he saw a woman named Bathsheba and decided to indulge his sexual passions. He later murdered her husband to cover his guilt (see 2 Samuel 11). He is not the one either.

In fact, the promised one won't be born until we enter the New Testament, though hints of his coming are littered throughout the Bible, like this passage in Isaiah:

> [1] *Who has believed our message*
> *and to whom has the arm of the LORD been revealed?*
> [2] *He grew up before him like a tender shoot,*
> *and like a root out of dry ground.*
> *He had no beauty or majesty to attract us to him,*
> *nothing in his appearance that we should desire him.*
> [3] *He was despised and rejected by mankind,*
> *a man of suffering, and familiar with pain.*
> *Like one from whom people hide their faces*
> *he was despised, and we held him in low esteem.*
>
> [4] *Surely he took up our pain*
> *and bore our suffering,*
> *yet we considered him punished by God,*
> *stricken by him, and afflicted.*
> [5] *But he was pierced for our transgressions,*
> *he was crushed for our iniquities;*
> *the punishment that brought us peace was on him,*
> *and by his wounds we are healed.*

⁶ *We all, like sheep, have gone astray,*

    each of us has turned to our own way;

and the Lord *has laid on him*

    the iniquity of us all.

⁷ *He was oppressed and afflicted,*

    yet he did not open his mouth;

he was led like a lamb to the slaughter,

    and as a sheep before its shearers is silent,

    so he did not open his mouth.

⁸ *By oppression and judgment he was taken away.*

    Yet who of his generation protested?

For he was cut off from the land of the living;

    for the transgression of my people he was punished.

⁹ *He was assigned a grave with the wicked,*

    and with the rich in his death,

though he had done no violence,

    nor was any deceit in his mouth.

¹⁰ *Yet it was the* Lord's *will to crush him and cause him to suffer,*

    and though the Lord *makes his life an offering for sin,*

he will see his offspring and prolong his days,

    and the will of the Lord *will prosper in his hand.*

¹¹ *After he has suffered,*

    he will see the light of life and be satisfied;

by his knowledge my righteous servant will justify many,

    and he will bear their iniquities.

¹² *Therefore I will give him a portion among the great,*

    and he will divide the spoils with the strong,

because he poured out his life unto death,

    and was numbered with the transgressors.

For he bore the sin of many,

    and made intercession for the transgressors.

Isaiah 53:1–12

3. What does Isaiah say about the one God will use to defeat Satan, sin, and death? What are at least three ways this passage gives you hope?

4. How do you respond to the fact that God had a plan from the foundation of the world to save your from sin and fix the world? What thoughts and emotions does this evoke?

God's Plan to Forgive Sin

Hundreds of years before Jesus' birth, prophets such as Isaiah were pointing forward to Christ as the fulfillment of the promise that God had made in Genesis 3:15. Jesus would not accomplish God's plan in the manner most expected—through military might or socio-political maneuvering. Rather, he would suffer and die, a reality hinted at when God said the snake would "strike [the] heel" of the promised one. But the seed of Eve would ultimately be victorious in a manner that would once and for all prove that he is God and vindicate the outworking of God's eternal plan to save sinners and fix the world. As Paul would later write:

20 Christ has indeed been raised from the dead, the firstfruits of those who have fallen asleep. 21 For since death came through a man, the resurrection of the dead comes also through a man. 22 For as in Adam all die, so in Christ all will be made alive. 23 But each in turn: Christ, the firstfruits; then, when he comes, those who belong to him. 24 Then the end will come, when he hands over the kingdom to God the Father after he has destroyed all dominion, authority and power. 25 For he must reign until he has put all his enemies under his feet. 26 The last enemy to be destroyed is death. 27 For he "has put everything under his feet."

1 Corinthians 15:20-27

God's promise of a child is accompanied by a picture of the way he will forgive sin. When Adam and Eve rebelled in the Garden, they immediately recognized they were naked and sought to cover their sin and shame with fig leaves (see Genesis 3:7). God saw them and judged them nonetheless, but that doesn't mean there was nothing that could cover their sin. For immediately after God issued the curse, he clothed Adam and Eve with the skins of a sacrificial animal whose blood had been shed to cover their sins (see Genesis 3:21).

The picture is clear. Because of sin, something has to die—either the sinner or a substitute. Since death is the consequence for sin, it makes sense that blood must be shed for one to be forgiven. The blood is a tangible sign that something has, in fact, died. This set a pattern that continued throughout the Old Testament, as the people offered animal sacrifices so their sins could be forgiven and they could have ongoing fellowship with God. But this changed with the arrival of Christ, as the following passage relates:

11 But when Christ came as high priest of the good things that are now already here, he went through the greater and more perfect tabernacle that is not made with human hands, that is to say, is not a part of this creation. 12 He did not enter by means of the blood of goats and calves; but he entered the Most Holy Place once for all by his own blood, thus obtaining eternal redemption. 13 The blood of goats and bulls and the ashes of a heifer sprinkled on those who

are ceremonially unclean sanctify them so that they are outwardly clean.
¹⁴ How much more, then, will the blood of Christ, who through the eternal Spirit
offered himself unblemished to God, cleanse our consciences from acts that
lead to death, so that we may serve the living God!

¹⁵ For this reason Christ is the mediator of a new covenant, that those who are
called may receive the promised eternal inheritance—now that he has died as
a ransom to set them free from the sins committed under the first covenant.

¹⁶ In the case of a will, it is necessary to prove the death of the one who made
it, ¹⁷ because a will is in force only when somebody has died; it never takes
effect while the one who made it is living. ¹⁸ This is why even the first covenant
was not put into effect without blood.

Hebrews 9:11–18

The key word in the book of Hebrews is *better.* The author holds up many of the concepts that defined the worship of Israel in the Old Testament and shows how Jesus is better than each one. In this passage, he states that Jesus offered a better sacrifice for sins because he offered his perfect life's blood once and for all, not repeatedly like the animal sacrifices in the Old Testament. Jesus' blood was sufficient to cover the sins of his people.

In God's plan, both the promise and the picture found in Genesis 3 are fulfilled in Christ. He fulfills both. He is the promised seed of Eve who crushed the serpent's head, and he is the sacrificial lamb who was sacrificed so that our sin could be covered.

5. Take a moment to reread Genesis 3:21. What do you notice about this verse? What does it reveal about God's love for you?

6. What does Paul say about Jesus' work in 1 Corinthians 15:20–27? What does the author of Hebrews state about Jesus' work in Hebrews 9:11–18?

REFLECT

The Greatness of God's Mercy

God had sufficient reason to leave the world in a state of hopelessness. Humanity had, after all, revolted against his love. The full extent of God's grace and kindness is rightly understood in the face of the depth of sin. The worse the situation, the more beautiful the love that is shown.

This reality is true in all life as well. For example, imagine a teenage girl who has been compliant with her parent's rules for the majority of time she has lived at home. But one night, she is hanging out with a friend and fails to check the time, which leads to her violating her curfew by five minutes. Her parents might be upset, but their daughter is probably not going to feel a huge sense of relief or indebtedness if they simply overlook her offense, remind her of the house rules, and ask her to be more responsible next time.

On the flip side, consider a teenage boy who has lived in constant rebellion since he entered adolescence. He constantly bucks his parents' authority and resists their rules. One weekend, he steals a credit card out of his mom's purse and takes off for the beach. After a night of partying and binge drinking, he is arrested for disorderly conduct and suspicion of driving while intoxicated. His parents are called to the beach to get him. He is guilty and truly deserves whatever punishment they might dole out.

But assume they show him grace and love in the face of this mess. The teenage boy is going to feel a greater sense of relief and indebtedness to his parents than did the teenage girl because of the gravity of his situation.

7. How should each of these teenagers respond to their parents' gift of grace?

8. When are times in your life that you have taken God's gift of grace for granted?

The Mission Continues

Love shines brightest against the darkest background. This is why we should spend time understanding the problem of human sin. The more we consider our sin nature and the outworking of that sin in our actions and throughout our culture, the better we are able to comprehend the amazing grace that we have been shown through God's answer to human sin. He had a promise and a plan all along. The more we dig into that truth, the more likely we are to overflow in praise and worship for the kindness and grace of God.

The story of Genesis 3 reveals that God is not finished with his people. Adam and Eve were not killed after their sin—though they could have been. They were banished from the Garden, but God allowed them to continue to live and multiply. In fact, Eve's name means "mother of all the living" (verse 20), which speaks to this reality.

The situation in which Adam and Eve found themselves did not come about because God had some morbid fascination to see them in pain—like a kid who steps on a bug to watch it slowly die. God was not simply sitting back and watching Adam and Eve live out their days before he would enact his sentence of death. He was not sitting back and allowing them to have kids who bore a replica of their sin nature so he could watch the world unravel. He allowed Adam and Eve to live because his mission would not be thwarted by human sin. He was never confused as to what to do next. In the face of sin, God was continually working out his plan of salvation through Christ so that his grace and love for his creation would be clear.

We know that God's mission did continue after the Fall, because it is reiterated even after sin enters the world. After the judgment of the flood in Genesis 7–8, God tells Noah and his sons to "be fruitful and increase in number and fill the earth" (9:1)—the same mission that God gave to Adam and Eve (see 1:28). Then, in Genesis 11, after God judges the people at the tower of Babel, he scatters them throughout the earth and confuses their language. They were meant to fill the earth with image-bearing worshipers of the one true God, but now they will fill the earth with the outworking of their sin nature. But God scatters them in order to accomplish his mission. What they won't do in obedience, he will make them do in judgment.

But then, as people fill the earth, those who respond in faith to God's plan are positioned to bear witness to his love and grace. Once again, they will live out their mission to make God's greatness known (see Matthew 28:19–20; Acts 1:8).

9. Read Ephesians 2:1–10. What does Paul say is wrong with the world?

10. What did God do to change this condition? What is your situation as a result?

CLOSE

"God . . . made us alive with Christ" (Ephesians 2:4–5). Everything changes with these words. Satan is defeated and the power of sin broken because God took the initiative to save us and fix the world. He did not leave us in our sin but pursued us in our brokenness and made a way for us to know, love, and live for him, just as we were created to do. The next chapter in God's story describes the outworking of this eternal plan that continues to this day. We are the unworthy recipients of the outworking of God's plan through the person of Jesus Christ.

11. What big ideas from *Revolt* have stuck with you? How have these truths changed the way you think about yourself, your world, and God?

12. Are you confident today that your sins are forgiven? If so, what gives you that security?

NEXT

In these six lessons of *Revolt,* we have seen how Adam and Eve's disobedience brought about judgment on humanity, created an irreparable separation between people and God, introduced a sin nature into every man and woman born on this earth, and ultimately created a system of evil in the world. But we have also seen how God—even while he was revealing the consequences of Adam and Eve's sin through the curse—was enacting a plan to redeem humanity and bring them back into a relationship with himself.

In *People,* the next study in this series, we will see how God continued to move this plan forward in spite of humanity's failings. We will explore how God, through a man named Abraham, commissioned a chosen people to be a witness of his faithfulness on earth. We will discover that even though this chosen race rejected him time and again, God was always faithful to show mercy to them when they repented and called on his name. But most importantly, we will see that at each turn of his people's cycle of rejection, repentance, and restoration, the Lord continued to announce his plan of salvation for the world.

Thank you for taking this journey! Stay the course. God has a lot that he wants to do in your life!

LEADER'S GUIDE

Thank you for your willingness to lead your group through this study. What you have chosen to do is valuable and will make a great difference in the lives of others. The rewards of being a leader are different from those of participating, and we hope that as you lead you will find your own walk with Jesus deepened by the experience.

The lessons in this study guide are suitable for church classes, Bible studies, and small groups. Each lesson is structured to provoke thought and help you grow in your knowledge and understanding of Christ. There are multiple components in this section that can help you structure your lessons and discussion time, so make sure you read and consider each one.

BEFORE YOU BEGIN

Before your first meeting, make sure the group members have a copy of this study guide so they can follow along and have their answers written out ahead of time. Alternately, you can hand out the study guides at your first meeting and give the group members some time to look over the material and ask any preliminary questions. During your first meeting, be sure to send a sheet of paper around the room and have the members write down their name, phone number, and email address so you can keep in touch with them during the week.

Generally, the ideal size for a group is eight to ten people, which will ensure that everyone has enough time to participate in discussions. If you have more people, you might want to break up the main group into smaller subgroups. Encourage those who show up at the first meeting to commit to attending the duration of the study. This will help the group members get to know one another, create stability for the group, and help you, as the leader, know how to best prepare each week.

Try to initiate a free-flowing discussion as you go through each lesson. Invite group members to bring any questions they have or insights they discover as they go through the content to the next meeting, especially if they were unsure of the meaning of some parts of the lesson. Be prepared to discuss the biblical truth that relates to each topic in the study.

WEEKLY PREPARATION

As the group leader, here are a few things you can do to prepare for each meeting:

- Make sure you understand the content of the lesson so you know how to structure group time and are prepared to lead group discussion.
- Depending on how much time you have each week, you may not be able to reflect on every question. Select specific questions that you feel will evoke the best discussion.
- At the end of your discussion, take prayer requests from your group members and pray for each other.

STRUCTURING THE DISCUSSION TIME

It is up to you to keep track of the time and keep things on schedule. You might want to set a timer for each question that you discuss so both you and the group members know when your time is up. (There are some good phone apps for timers that play a gentle chime or other pleasant sound instead of a disruptive noise.)

Don't be concerned if the group members are quiet or slow to share. People are often quiet when they are pulling together their ideas, and this might be a new experience for them. Just ask a question and let it hang in the air until someone shares. You can then say, "Thank you. What about others? What thoughts came to you?"

If you need help in organizing your time when planning your group Bible study, the following schedule, for sixty minutes and ninety minutes, can give you a structure for the lesson:

	60 Minutes	90 Minutes
Welcome: Arrive and get settled	5 minutes	10 minutes
Message: Review the lesson	15 minutes	25 minutes
Discussion: Discuss study questions	35 minutes	45 minutes
Prayer: Pray together and dismiss	5 minutes	10 minutes

GROUP DYNAMICS

Leading a group through *Revolt* will prove to be highly rewarding both to you and your group members. But you still may encounter challenges along the way! Discussions can get off track. Group members may not be sensitive to the needs and ideas of others. Some might worry they will be expected to talk about matters that make them feel awkward. Others may express comments that result in disagreements. To help ease this strain on you and the group, consider the following ground rules:

- When someone raises a question or comment that is off the main topic, suggest you deal with it another time, or, if you feel led to go in that direction, let the group know you will be spending some time discussing it.

- If someone asks a question that you don't know how to answer, admit it and move on. At your discretion, feel free to invite group members to comment on questions that call for personal experience.

- If you find one or two people are dominating the discussion time, direct a few questions to others in the group. Outside the main group time, ask the more dominating members to help you draw out the quieter ones. Work to make them a part of the solution instead of the problem.

- When a disagreement occurs, encourage the group members to process the matter in love. Encourage those on opposite sides to restate what they heard the other side say about the matter, and then invite each side to evaluate if that perception is accurate. Lead the group in examining other Scriptures related to the topic and look for common ground.

When any of these issues arise, encourage your group members to follow these words from the Bible: "Love one another" (John 13:34), "If it is possible, as far as it depends on you, live at peace with everyone" (Romans 12:18), "Whatever is true . . . noble . . . right . . . if anything is excellent or praiseworthy—think about such things" (Philippians 4:8), and "Be quick to listen, slow to speak and slow to become angry" (James 1:19). This will make your group time more rewarding and beneficial for everyone who attends.

Thank you again for your willingness to lead your group. May God reward your efforts and dedication, equip you to guide your group in the weeks ahead, and make your time together fruitful for his kingdom.

ABOUT THE AUTHORS

Aaron Coe is the founder and CEO of Future City Now, a strategy consulting firm that helps executive leaders maximize their influence on the world. He and his wife, Carmen, have been involved in the Passion Movement for more than twenty years and currently serve as the leaders of the Trilith location of Passion City Church. Aaron has a Ph.D. in Applied Theology and teaches at Dallas Theological Seminary. Additionally, Aaron served as the General Editor of *The Jesus Bible*. Aaron and Carmen live in the Atlanta area with their four children.

Matt Rogers holds a Ph.D. in Applied Theology and teaches and writes on Christian mission, ministry, and discipleship. Notably, Matt served as the lead writer for the bestselling *The Jesus Bible*. He and his wife, Sarah, and their five children live in Greenville, South Carolina, where Matt serves as the pastor of Christ Fellowship Cherrydale.

The Jesus Bible Study Series

Beginnings
ISBN 9780310154983
On sale January 2023

Revolt
ISBN 9780310155003
On sale May 2023

People
ISBN 9780310155027
On sale September 2023

Savior
ISBN 9780310155041
On sale January 2024

Church
ISBN 9780310155065
On sale May 2024

Forever
ISBN 9780310155089
On sale September 2024

Available wherever books are sold

The Jesus Bible

sixty-six books. one story. all about one name.

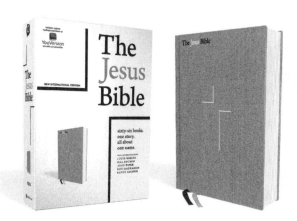

The Jesus Bible, NIV & ESV editions, with feature essays from Louie Giglio, Max Lucado, John Piper, and Randy Alcorn, as well as profound yet accessible study features will help you meet Jesus throughout Scripture.

- 350 full page articles
- 700 side-bar articles
- Book introductions
- Room for journaling

The Jesus Bible Journal, NIV
Study individual books of the Bible featuring lined journal space and commentary from *The Jesus Bible.*

- 14 journals covering 30 books of the Bible
- 2 boxed sets (OT & NT)

TheJesusBible.com

Video Study for Your Church or Small Group

In this six-session video Bible study, bestselling author and pastor Louie Giglio helps you apply the principles in *Don't Give the Enemy a Seat at Your Table* to your life. The study guide includes access to six streaming video sessions, video notes and a comprehensive structure for group discussion time, and personal study for deeper reflection between sessions.

Study Guide + Streaming Video
9780310156284

DVD
9780310134268

Available now at your favorite bookstore
or streaming video on StudyGateway.com.

It's Not the Height
of the Giant
...but the Size of
Our God

Study Guide + Streaming Video
9780310146506

DVD
9780310083764

EXPLORE THE PRINCIPLES IN *GOLIATH MUST FALL* WITH YOUR small group through this six-session video-based study. Each week, pastor Louie Giglio will provide practical steps and biblical principles for how you and your group can defeat the "giants" in your lives like fear, rejection, comfort, anger, or addiction. Includes discussion questions, Bible exploration, and personal study materials for in between sessions.